THE BOOK OF

revelation

(A NEW TRANSLATION)

Translation © Michael Straus (2017), from the text published as
B. Aland, K. Aland, J. Karavidopoulos, C. M. Martini and B. M. Metzger (eds.),
The Greek New Testament (5th edition) (Stuttgart: German Bible Society, 2014)

Illustrations © Jennifer May Reiland (2017), from her drawings
"Self Portrait as Mary Magdalene Having a Vision of the Apocalypse I" (2015) and
"Self Portrait as Mary Magdalene Having a Vision of the Apocalypse II" (2015)"

Design: Practical People

ISBN 978-1-944682-85-9
Description: New York City : Spuyten Duyvil, 2018.
Identifiers: LCCN 2017033124 | ISBN 9781944682859 (pbk.)
Classification: LCC BS2823 .S77 2018 | DDC 228/.05209-- dc23
LC record available at https://lccn.loc.gov/2017033124

THE BOOK OF

revelation

(A NEW TRANSLATION)

TRANSLATION BY MICHAEL STRAUS
ILLUSTRATIONS BY JENNIFER MAY REILAND

Hidden things are now revealed, God putting it in Jesus' hands to disclose these secrets to his servants so they will be ready for what's about to happen. And God himself sent this revelation to me, his servant John, confirming it by way of an angel messenger. I therefore here bear witness to the Word of God and the testimony of Jesus Christ and to all that I learned by sight and by sound. Anyone who reads or hears the words of this prophetic book—and guards it safe in her heart—will be multiply blessed, for the very moment is upon us.

Watch! For he comes with clouds and all will see on him, even those who pierced him, and all the tribes of the Earth will beat their breasts because of him. Listen to me—that's just what will happen.

"I am Ἄλφα and Ὠμέγα, he who was and is and is to come, the Almighty God," says the Lord.

I your brother John share not only in your suffering but also in the kingdom and patience of Jesus and I write now from the island called Patmos, an exile for the Word of God and my testimony concerning the Savior. As I worshipped there on the Lord's Day I was caught up to see things unseen, hear things unheard, filled with the Spirit and a vision of Heaven.

So let me start with the message I was given to the seven churches in the Asian Province, bringing grace and peace from God who is and was and is to come and from the seven Spirits in perfect plenitude before his throne and from Jesus Christ, the faithful witness, first-born from among the dead and ruler of all the kings of the Earth. Now to him who loved us and redeemed us from our sins by his own blood and made us kings and priests to God and his Father, to him be everlasting glory and power. Amen.

The first thing I heard seemed to be a great voice behind me sounding as if it were a trumpet saying "Write what you are seeing on a scroll and send it to the seven churches, even to Ephesus and to Smyrna and to Pergamos and to Thyatira and to Sardis and to Philadelphia and to Laodicea."

Turning around to see the voice speaking I gazed on gilt candlesticks seven where among the candlesticks I saw someone seeming like the Son of Man–tall in copious white of Zahar wool he stood belted with the gold of Uphaz across his chest his head and hairs white like snow his eyes as wheels two flames flashing his feet fine brass fresh from the furnace his voice a flood surrounding me like rushing streams seven stars within his right hand a keen two-edged sword issuing from his mouth his countenance like the dawn fair as the moon radiant as the sun majestic as the star. in procession–and I fell at his feet as though dead.

But he his right hand laid upon me said, "Don't be afraid! I am the First and the Last, the Living One. Though I died, look! I am forever living and hold the keys of Doom and Destruction. Write down now what you've seen–things that are and things that will be. Listen first to the secret of the seven stars seen in my right hand and the seven golden candlesticks–the seven stars are the angels of the seven churches, the seven candlesticks the seven churches themselves.

"Therefore write this to the messenger of the church at Ephesus: Hear what the one holding seven stars fast in his right hand says, the same one walking in the midst of the seven golden candlesticks–I know your deeds, your toil, your patience, your intolerance for the wicked. same one walking in the midst of the seven golden candlesticks—I know your deeds, your toil, your patience, your intolerance for the wicked. I know you have tested the spirits of those who call themselves apostles but are not and found them to be liars. And I know you have endured and labored for my name's sake and not grown weary. But still I've put a mark against you in my book because you've left behind your first love. Remember those earlier days, think whence you've fallen—and then turn back and tend to first things first lest failing I come swiftly to seize your candlestick from its holder. But I grant you this: you hate those who oppress the people, those I too despise. Let all who have ears hear what the Spirit says to the churches. To her who overcomes will I grant to eat from the Tree of Life, the Tree in the Paradise of my God.

"Write this to the messenger of the church at Smyrna: This is what the First and Last says, he who was dead and is alive—I know your deeds, your pains, your poverty (and yet you are rich!) and I know the sacrilege of those contesting for Israel's heart even as they worship her foe. Though the Accuser stands guard at the gates of your prison, ten days of torment held in his hand, yet fear not the things you'll suffer. Be faithful if need be even unto death and I'll hand you the Crown of Life. Let those who have ears hear what the Spirit says to the churches. Whoever conquers will never be harmed by the second death.

"And write this to the messenger of the church in Pergamos: This is what the one who holds the sharp and double-edged sword says—I know your deeds and where you dwell, even in the Tempter's home town. Yet you've held fast to my name not denying my faith even in the days when my faithful martyr Antipas was murdered in your midst, yes, right there where Beelzebub thinks he's safe. But even so, I have ayes, right there

where Beelzebub thinks he's safe. But even so, I have a few things against you because some of you hold to Balaam's doctrine, he who taught Balak to cast a snare on the children of Israel—that they should eat things sacrificed to idols and commit adultery. And you also have some among you siding with the people's oppressors, something you know I hate. I tell you turn from all that, lest failing I come swiftly to fight against them with the sword of my mouth. Let those who have ears hear what the Spirit says to the churches. To him who overcomes will I grant to eat of the Hidden Manna—and I will give him a white stone with a new name written on it, a name no one knows but the one who receives it.

"And to the messenger of the church at Thyatira write: This is what the Son of God says, whose eyes are like a flame of fire, whose feet are like fine brass fired in a furnace—I know your deeds and love and faith and service and patience, yes, and your latest deeds, which are even greater than your first. Yet I still have something against you because you tolerate that woman Jezebel—she calls herself a prophet even as by wiles she leads my servants into lechery and idolatry. I gave her space to repent but she would not, so mired she was in her own whorishness. Therefore I will toss her to a bed—and her adulterous partners with her—there to suffer great torment unless they turn away from her deeds; and I will also put her children to death. Let all the churches know that I pierce to the innermost thoughts and soul—I will reward each of you according to your deeds. But I say to you and the rest in Thyatira—all who abhor her teaching, who have not plumbed the deep things of the Evil One—I will not cast any greater burden on you than this: hold fast to what you have until I come. To him who overcomes and guards my works 'til the end will I give the nations to be his inheritance and he will break them with a rod of iron and dash them to pieces like a potter's vessel—just as I have received power from my Father—and I will give him the Morning Star. Let those who have ears hear what the Spirit says to the churches.

"And to the messenger of the church at Sardis write: This is what the one who holds the seven Spirits of God and the seven stars says—I know your deeds, that you have the reputation of being alive, but are dead. Wake up! Strengthen what's left and is about to die, for I've found your deeds wanting before the face of my God. Call to mind all that you've received and all that you've heard—guard it closely and turn from your ways. If you will not awake, if you will not watch, I will come as thief—you won't even know the hour I come for you. Even so, there are some named among you in Sardis who have not stained their robes—they will walk with me in white, for they are worthy. I will drape fair garments on those who overcome and never wipe their names from the Book of Life, but will confess their names before my Father and before his angels. Let those who have ears hear what the Spirit says to the churches.

"And to the messenger of the church at Philadelphia write: This is what the Holy One says, the True, who keeps the Key of the House of David, who having opened no one closes and having closed no one opens—I know your deeds and behold, I have opened a door before you, one that no one can close, because I know that you have but little strength left—for you have kept my word and never denied my name. And what of those who pretend to be true Children of Israel but lie and aren't. They're the Devil's own parishioners and I will have them lie prostrate at your feet, so that they know I have loved you. But because you have patiently endured, guarding my word with steadfastness, I—even I—will keep you safe from the hour of trial, that time soon to fall upon the whole world to try those who dwell upon the Earth. I will come swiftly. Hold tight to what you have. Let no one steal your crown. She who overcomes will be a pillar in the temple of my God. She will dwell there forever and I will write on her the name of my God and the name of the city of my God—the new Jerusalem, which comes down from my God in Heaven—and I will write upon her my new name. Let soon to fall upon the whole world to try those who dwell upon the Earth. I will come swiftly. Hold tight to what you have. Let no one steal your crown. She who overcomes will be a pillar in the temple of my God. She will dwell there forever and I will write on her the name of my God and the name of the city of my God–the new Jerusalem, which comes down from my God in Heaven–and I will write upon her my new name. Let those who have ears hear what the Spirit says to the churches.

"And to the messenger of the church at Laodicea write: This is what the Amen says, the Faithful and True Witness, the Beginning of the Creation of God–I know your deeds, that you are neither frigid nor hot, yet I wish you were one or the other. But because you are merely tepid–not hot, not cold–I'm about to spit you out of my mouth. But you say 'I am wealthy, I've gotten rich, I need nothing.' You have no idea that you are in fact wretched, miserable, poor, blind and naked. I urge you to buy from me gold, pure, refined (then you will truly be rich); and white robes (then will you be well-clothed indeed, covering the shame of your nakedness); and salve to anoint your eyes (then you will truly see). I only reprove and chasten those whom I love, so be zealous, and turn from your ways. Look! I stand striking at the door–if anyone hears my voice and opens the door I will enter and dine with him and he with me. Whoever overcomes will sit with me on my throne–I myself also conquered and now am seated with my Father on his throne. Let those who have ears hear what the Spirit says to the churches."

Looking again–behold!–I saw an open door appear in Heaven and the first voice I heard speaking to me sounding something like a trumpet said "Come up here and I will show you things yet to happen."

Then!

As in night visions even in an instant I was in the Spirit seeing before me a throne at Heaven's Gate the countenance of him upon it appearing clear as jasper blood-red as Sardian stone an emerald iris encircling the throne encircling again twice twelvefold thrones on them two dozen elders sitting wrapped radiant in purest white robes gleaming upon their heads crowns of gold and from the throne lightning bolts and thunder peals beneath the throne seven burning lamps blazing—these the seven Spirits of God—before the throne a glass sea shimmering as if it were rock crystal in the midst of the throne circling about it four living creatures eyes covering them front and back the first like a lion the second an ox the third a man the fourth a soaring eagle each creature having six wings with eyes wheeling within wheels ceaselessly singing day and night

>   Sanctus, Sanctus, Sanctus

>   Dominus Deus omnipotens .

>   qui erat, et qui est, et qui venturus est.

And as the four living creatures gave endless glory and honor and praise to him forever living who sits upon the throne so too the four and twenty elders fell down before the Ancient of Days eternally worshipping him who lives forever casting crowns woven of amaranth and gold before the throne singing

>   You are worthy O Holy Lord and our God

>>   to receive glory and honor and power

>   for you created all things

>>   and by your word they are and were created.

Then!

I saw lying on the open right hand of the one seated on the throne a scroll fully written inside and out but tightly sealed with seven seals as a mighty angel cried with a loud voice "Who is worthy to open the scroll and to loose its seals?" But no angels in Heaven no people on the Earth nor dead below the Earth had the power to open the book or even to gaze upon it. So I for my part cried, shedding no end of tears when I heard there was none found worthy so much as to look upon the scroll, let alone to loose its seals. But one from among the elders said to me "Weep not, for look! The Lion of the Tribe of Judah has prevailed, the Root of Jesse, the Branch of David—and he will break open the seven seals, revealing all that is in the scroll."

And then there appeared to me standing in the midst of the throne amidst the four living creatures amidst the twenty-four elders a Lamb as sacrifice slain throat sliced having seven horns and seven eyes—these the seven Spirits of God sent through all the Earth—approaching taking the scroll from the one seated on the throne the four living creatures the four and twenty elders falling before the Lamb each having a stringed instrument and golden bowls filled with incense—these the prayers of the Holy Ones—this new song singing

>You are worthy to take the scroll
>
>>and break open its seals
>
>because you were slain
>
>>and with your own blood redeemed
>
>from every tribe and tongue and race and nation
>
>>a people for God
>
>e ne hai fatto per il nostro Dio un regno e dei sacerdoti—
>
>>e regneranno sulla terra.

Watching still I heard the sound of myriad angels surrounding the throne and the creatures and the elders their number ten thousand ten thousands a thousand thousands over again in choral voice praising as they sang with might

    Worthy is the Lamb that was slain

        to receive power and riches

    and wisdom and strength

        and honor and glory and blessing!

Even still again I heard all angels in Heaven all people on the Earth and the dead below the Earth and every creature upon the sea and all those in Earth and sea answering saying

    Soient louange et honneur,

        glory and power

    al que está sentado en el trono

        y al Cordero in sæcula sæculorum.

And I heard once more the four living creatures say "Amen" and saw the elders fall upon their faces worshipping.

Still watching I saw the Lamb open one of the seven seals and one of the four living creatures speaking as thunder roars said "Come!" and I beheld a white horse one upon it with a bow given power to go conquering that he might conquer then the Lamb opened the second seal the second living creature said "Come!" and another horse this time red and upon it one with a mighty sword taking peace away from the Earth men murdering men then the Lamb opened the third seal and the third living creature said "Come!" and I saw a black horse upon it one with a pair of

scales in his hand while a sound from the midst of the four living creatures spoke saying "A day's pay for a pound of wheat, a day's pay for three pounds of barley, yet leave no shortage of oil and wine" then the Lamb opened the fourth seal and the sound of the fourth living creature said "Come!" and I saw a horse green in pallor one atop it having the name Death all Hell following him with power killing a quarter of Earth's people with slashing Thracian blade famine death ravaging wild beasts and even so the Lamb opened the fifth seal and looking I saw below the altar the souls of all slaughtered for the sake of the Word of God and the testimony and cried out together with great voice saying "How much longer Holy Master and True until you judge vindicating our blood upon all who dwell on the Earth?" each one wearing a white robe long and glistening and told patiently to wait a little while longer until their ranks be complete continuously filling up with their fellow servants' souls the souls of their brothers and sisters yet to be slain as were they but when the Lamb opened the sixth seal seismic shudders seized the Earth the sun as sackcloth darkening the whole moon turning to blood the stars of Heaven falling to Earth as late Summer figs wind-shaken the whole Heaven splitting apart rolling up as a scroll every mountain and island upended from its roots the kings of the Earth the rulers the captains the rich the strong all slaves and all free hiding themselves in mountain dens and stone grottos crying out to the mountains and the rocks "Fall on us and hide us from the face of the one who sits on the throne and from the wrath of the Lamb for the Great Day of his wrath is come and who can withstand it?"

Yet again transfixed I saw four angels standing at the four corners of the Earth holding fast the Four Winds lest they blow upon the land or the seas or even any tree while another angel rising with the rising of the sun holding the seal of the living God with great voice calling to the four angels having power to ravish land and sea said "Touch not the land nor sea nor even any tree until we have sealed the servants of our God upon their foreheads." I heard the number of those being sealed, 144,000, sealed from every tribe of the sons of Israel: from the tribe of Judah 12,000, from the tribe of Reuben 12,000, from the tribe of Gad 12,000, from the tribe of Asher 12,000, from the tribe of Nephtali 12,000, from the tribe of Manasseh 12,000, from the tribe of Simeon 12,000, from the tribe of Levi 12,000, from the tribe of Issachar 12,000, from the tribe of Zebulon 12,000, from the tribe of Joseph 12,000 and from the tribe of Benjamin 12,000.

And watching I saw a vast crowd from all nations and tribes and peoples and tongues numberless uncountable by anyone standing before the throne and before the Lamb together robed gleaming white palm branches in their hands waving in joyous shout proclaiming

>Salus Deo nostro

>qui sedet super thronum et Agno.

So too the angels gathered about the throne the elders the four living creatures all falling face down before the throne worshipping God singing

>Amen! Praise and glory and wisdom
>>and blessing and honor and power and strength be to our

>God for all endless ages.

Then one of the elders said to me asking, "Who are these gathered in glistering white robes and whence have they come?" But I answered, "My lord, do you know?" So he told me, "These are they who have passed through the great suffering and washed their garments and made them white in the blood of the Lamb. Therefore they stand day and night before the throne of God worshipping him in his temple and he who sits upon the throne has his tabernacle among them. They no longer hunger nor thirst and the sun's scorching heat falls not upon them–for the Lamb in the midst of the throne is their shepherd, leading them beside the still waters–and God himself blots every tear away from their eyes."

But when the Lamb broke open the seventh seal silence held Heaven as for half an hour and looking I saw the seven angels who stand before God holding seven trumpets and another angel standing by the sacrificial altar before the throne holding a golden censer filled with incense offering it together with the prayers of the Holy Ones uponthe auric altar before the throne smoke rising up before God from the hand of the angel offering the incense the angel also taking the censer filling it with fiery ashes from the altar casting it upon the Earth–and there came thunder, roaring, lightning, quakes.

And then the seven angels with the seven trumpets poised to sound.

The first sounded his trumpet and hail and fire mingled with blood showered the Earth burning a third of the Earth and a third of all trees and all green grass the second angel echoed and as it were a great mountain smoldering lit with fire was hurled to the sea the third part of the sea turning to blood killing the living creatures sinking the ships as the third angel blew his trumpet a great and glowing star like to a torch fell from the Heavens on a third of the rivers and springs of waters–this star has a name and its name is Absinthe–and a third of the waters turned to wormwood myriads dying from the embittered waters the fourth angel

trumpeting blotted out the third part of the sun and the third part of the moon and the third part of the stars eclipsing their light the day blackening a third so also the night.

As I looked I saw and heard an angel soaring like an eagle through the midst of Heaven crying aloud "Woe, woe, woe to those who dwell upon the Earth for the blasts of the three angels' trumpets yet to sound."

Then when the fifth angel sounded I saw the star fallen as lightning from Heaven to Earth holding in his hand the key to Hell's wide well uncovering that pit of gloom soot rose up the shaft as through the stack of an iron furnace veiling the sun even the air itself with the infernal smoke while locust-like creatures emerged from the cloud shrouding the Earth with power to sting as a scorpion stings—but they were told not to harm the grasslands or any pale plant or any tree only thoseshrouding the Earth with power to sting as a scorpion stings—but they were told not to harm the grasslands or any pale plant or any tree only those men who bore not God's seal upon their heads yet neither should they kill them rather torture five months tormenting them with a scorpion's burning strike. Men will seek death rather than suffer those days of travail but not find it, yearn to die but find death fled from them. Now the shapes of these swarming creatures were as horses ready for war but with faces like men their heads seemingly crowned in gold yet with hair like women teeth as a lion's breasts covered with iron plates—or so was the likeness—with the semblance of wings making a sound as would horse-drawn chariots massed rushing to battle. And they had scorpions' tails—or what appeared to be stingers—able to plague men five months with their fiery strikes. Their king was the messenger of the Abyss, whose name in Greek is Ἀπολλύων but in English—the Destroyer. One woe is past but two remain.

When the sixth angel sounded his trumpet, I heard a single voice come from the four horns of the golden altar that stands before God saying to the sixth angel holding its trumpet, "Release the four angels who lie bound in the great River Euphrates!" And so these four angels were set free, having been prepared for this very hour and day and month and year, prepared to kill a third of all mankind. Their horsemen numbered twice ten thousand ten thousands—I heard their number—seemingly breast-plated in fire dipped in sulphur the color of blue-blooded Hyacinth their horses having lions' heads mouths vomiting fire and smoke and sulphur with breath three times a plague of burning brimstone blotting out a third of human life—for the horses' power lay in their mouths and in their tails a viper's sting.

And yet the rest of mankind, all those who survived these woes, still did not turn from their evil deeds, not from their worship of demons and idols—things made of gold and silver and bronze and wood and stone that cannot see or hear or walk—not even from murder, sorcery, perversion and theft.

Then I saw another angel, powerful, descending cloud-clothed from Heaven the brightness around him as the image of God's bow appears in light rain his face a solar blaze his feet two flame pillars holding in his right hand a small scroll unrolled placing his right foot upon the sea his left upon the land shouting with a voice loud as a lion's roar—and as he cried out seven thunders spoke. When they finished speaking I was poised to write down their words but heard a voice from Heaven command me saying, "Seal up what the seven thunders spoke and write it not!" Then the Colossus straddling land and sea lifted his right hand to Heaven and swore by him who lives all ages forever, who created Heaven and all that is in it and Earth and all that is in it and the sea and all that is in it saying, "Time shall be no more, but in the days of the seventh angel's voice when he is about to sound his trumpet God's hidden mystery shall be complete, the good news foretold by God to his servants the prophets."

The voice I heard from Heaven spoke to me again and said, "Go, take the opened small scroll from the hand of the angel spanning land and sea." So I went to the angel and said, "Hand me the small scroll." He said to me, "Take and eat—it will be sweet as honey in your mouth but bitter to your stomach." Then I took the small scroll from the angel's hand and ate it whole. It was sweet tasting to my mouth but, when I was done, bitter to my belly. He told me, "You must prophesy again to many peoples and nations and tongues and kings."

Then he gave me a measuring rod, something like a staff, and said, "Rise up and go take measure of the temple of God and the altar and those who worship there. But do not measure the court outside the temple, for it has been given to the Gentile nations and they will trample the holy city for 42 months. Yet I will give power to my two witnesses and they will prophesy for 1,260 days, clothed in sackcloth. These are the two olives trees and the two candlesticks that stand before the Prince of this World. Should anyone have a mind to harm them fire from their mouths will burn their enemies to a crisp—and anyone seeking to injure them must be killed in that manner. They have power to lock the doors of Heaven and to stop the rain from falling all the days of their prophecy. So too they have power to turn the waters to blood and to strike the Earth with every sort of plague, so often as they wish. And when their testimony is complete the beast ascending from the Depth will go to war with them and defeat them and kill them.

"Their corpses will lie on the main boulevard of the great city, spiritually named Sodom and Egypt, where also their Lord was crucified. And for three and a half days people from all regions and tribes and tongues

and nations will gaze at their bodies and not let anyone bury them in a tomb—Earth's inhabitants will rejoice in their deaths and celebrate, sending presents to one another, because these two prophets tormented those who dwell upon the Earth. But after three and a half days God breathed upon the slain and they stood on their feet—and a vast terror fell upon all who saw them. Then they heard a mighty voice from Heaven speak to them saying, 'Come up here!'. And they ascended to Heaven in a cloud, their enemies watching. In that same hour the Earth shook and a tenth of the city collapsed, the quake killing seven thousand souls—but the rest in fear gave glory to God in Heaven."

God in Heaven." Two woes have passed but one remains.

When the seventh angel sounded his trumpet deep voices vast spoke from Heaven saying

> The kingdom of the world is now become
>> the kingdom of our Lord and his Anointed—
> and he shall reign forever and ever.

And the four and twenty elders who sit on their thrones before God fell upon their faces and worshipped God saying

> We give thanks to you, Lord God Almighty
>> because you have seized your great power
> and taken rule.
>> The nations were angered
> but the time of your wrath has come
>> and with it judgment over all who have died—

> rewards to your servants the prophets
>
> and to all holy ones,
>
> those who fear your name both small and great,
>
> but destruction to Earth's destroyers.

Then the temple of God was opened in Heaven and in it the Ark of his Covenant—and there appeared lightning, voices, thunderclaps, tremors, hailstones.

Then too appeared a marvelous sign in Heaven—a sun-draped woman, the moon below her feet, her head crowned with twelve stars, at full term crying out in her birth pains. And another sign appeared, immense, a fire-red dragon with seven crowned heads and ten horns, his tail sweeping a third of the stars casting them down to Earth. He stood before the woman as she was about to give birth in the hope of devouring the child when it was born. And she did give birth, to a male child, one destined to rule all nations with an iron scepter. But the child was snatched away to God and his throne while the woman fled into the desert, where she has a place prepared for her by God, being nourished there 1,260 days.

There was war in Heaven, Michael and his angels battling the dragon. The dragon and his angels fought back but they were no match and forfeited their place in Heaven. So the great dragon was cast out, that old snake, the one they call Lucifer, El Diablo, the whole world's deceiver—he was hurled down to Earth and his legions with him.

Then a voice resounding in Heaven said

> Now is come the salvation and power and kingdom of God
>
> and the power of his Anointed
>
> because the Accuser of our brethren is cast down,
>
> he who slandered them before God day and night—
>
> for they have triumphed over him by the blood of the Lamb
>
> and the word of their testimony
>
> and they loved not their own souls, even to death.
>
> Therefore rejoice O Heavens and all who dwell therein.
>
> But woe to the land and sea:
>
> for the Devil comes down to you in fiercest rage,
>
> knowing his days are numbered.

So the dragon being cast down to Earth persecuted the woman who gave birth to the male child. On wide eagle wings the woman flew to her safe place in the desert, where she was nourished for a season and seasons and half a season from the face of that serpent. But the viper spewed water from his mouth like a flood, pursuing the woman, hoping to sweep her away in the tide. Yet the land gave her succor, opening its mouth and swallowing up the water the dragon cast from its mouth. And again the dragon fumed against the woman and battled the rest of her line—these are they who guard the commandments of God and hold fast their witness an Tiarna Íosa.

And as I stood at the shoreline I saw a beast ascend from the sea with ten crowned horns and seven heads and on each head a blasphemous name written, this beast in form like a leopard—save for its bear's paws and lion's mouth. The dragon gave its own power and throne to the beast, granting him great sway. It appeared as though one of the beast's heads had been slain, but the deathblow healed and the whole Earth marveled at the beast and they knelt to worship the dragon because it had given authority to the beast. So too they bowed down before the beast saying, "Who is like unto the beast and who is able to fight against him?"

The Lawless One was given space for his blasphemies, holding power for 42 months, opening his mouth to belch curses against God, profaning his name and his tabernacle and all those who dwell in Heaven. And the Antichrist went to war against os santos de Deus, defeating them, ruling over every tribe and people and tongue and nation, all worshipping him—those, that is, whose names were not written in the Lamb's Book of Life, he who was slain from the beginning of the world.

If anyone has ears, let him hear.

Anyone who takes a captive will be taken captive and anyone who lives by the sword will die by the sword. Herein lies the faith and patience of the saints.

Yet another beast I saw rising up from the Earth. He had two horns that looked like a lamb's but he spoke with a dragon's voice. He had all the authority of the first beast, wielding it in his presence, and he made all the inhabitants of the Earth worship the first beast, the one whose seemingly mortal wound was healed. This second beast performed great wonders, even making fire fall on men from Heaven, deceiving Earth's people by the signs he did in the beast's name, commanding them to fashion an image of beast—who though wounded with a sword still lived.

And he gave breath to the image of the Son of Perdition so that it spoke and he had power to put to death any who would not worship the image. Then he forced all, small and great, rich and poor, free and slave, to be sealed on the right hand or the forehead with the graven image of the beast. Without that mark they could neither buy nor sell. And the mark is the name of the beast, or the number of his name. But mark this wisdom and let anyone with his wits about him count the number of the beast, for it's a man's number—666.

Again I turned and saw the Lamb, this time standing on Mount Zion with 144,000 souls and written upon their foreheads I saw his name and the name of his Father. Then I heard a voice from Heaven as a noise of roiling waterswith 144,000 souls and written upon their foreheads I saw his name and the name of his Father. Then I heard a voice from Heaven as a noise of roiling waters rumbling on like thunder while these souls lyric as minstrel bards lifting their voices in chorus sang a new hymn before the throne and before the four living creatures and before the elders—and no one could learn the song save the 144,000 souls rescued from the Earth, chaste youths following the Lamb wherever he might go, redeemed as first-fruits harvested of mankind for God and the Lamb, blameless, in whose mouths no lies were found.

Then I saw a messenger of the eternal evangel winging through the midst of Heaven spreading the good news to all those dwelling upon the Earth and upon the sea and to every nation and tribe and tongue and people heralding with deeply sonorous voice, "Stand in awe of God and give him glory because the hour of his judgment is come: worship therefore him who made Heaven and Earth and the sea and all springs of water."

Yet again another angel, this second one following said, "Alas, Babylon—Babylon that great city is fallen, for she poured out to every nation the raging wine of her adultery."

And then another following them, this third cried out and said, "If anyone should worship the beast and his image and take upon his forehead or upon his right hand the mark of the beast he, even he will drink the unadulterated wine of judgment poured into the cup of God's wrath and be tormented in sulphur and smoke before the holy angels and the Lamb. The smoke of their torment shall rise up ages without end–day and night they have no surcease of sorrow, those who worshipped the beast and his likeness, those who took to themselves the image of his name."

Herein lies the patience of the saints, who guard the commandments of God, keeping the faith of Yeshua. Then I heard a voice from Heaven saying, "Write! Blessed are the dead, all who die in the Lord henceforth." The Spirit too said, "Amen, so may they rest from their labors, and their deeds shall follow them."

I gazed, and behold!–a white cloud and one seated on the cloud seeming like the Son of Man having a golden crown upon his head and in his hand a sharp sickle and another messenger coming out from within the temple calling with a loud voice to the one seated on the cloud, "Put forth your sickle and reap, for the harvest time is come and the crop is about to wither." So he who sat upon the cloud thrust his sickle into the Earth and the Earth was harvested.

Another angel emerged from Heaven's temple and he too had a sharp sickle, while yet another angel came forth from the altar having power over fire and crying with a loud voice to the first one holding the sharp sickle saying, "Lay out your sickle and gather in the grapes from Earth's vines, for the clusters are ripe."

So the angel thrust his sickle into the Earth and cast the grapes into the great winepress of God's anger and as the grapes of wrath were trampled down blood flowed from the press spreading 200 miles beyond the city, even reaching the height of horses' bits.

Then passing wondrous I saw a sign in Heaven seven angels with seven last plagues wrapping full the wrath of God.

And I beheld as it were a sea of glass laced with fire and on it standing those victorious over the beast and the number of his name holding in their hands God's lyres singing the song of Moses the servant of God and the song of the Lamb

>Great and wondrous are your deeds

>>O Seigneur Dieu, Tout-Puissant,

>just and true are your paths

>>O Rei de la Nacío!

>Who dares not reverence you, Señor,

>>who dares not give you the glory?

>For you alone are holy–

>>so the Goyim shall come

>and worship before you,

>>for your righteousness has been fully revealed.

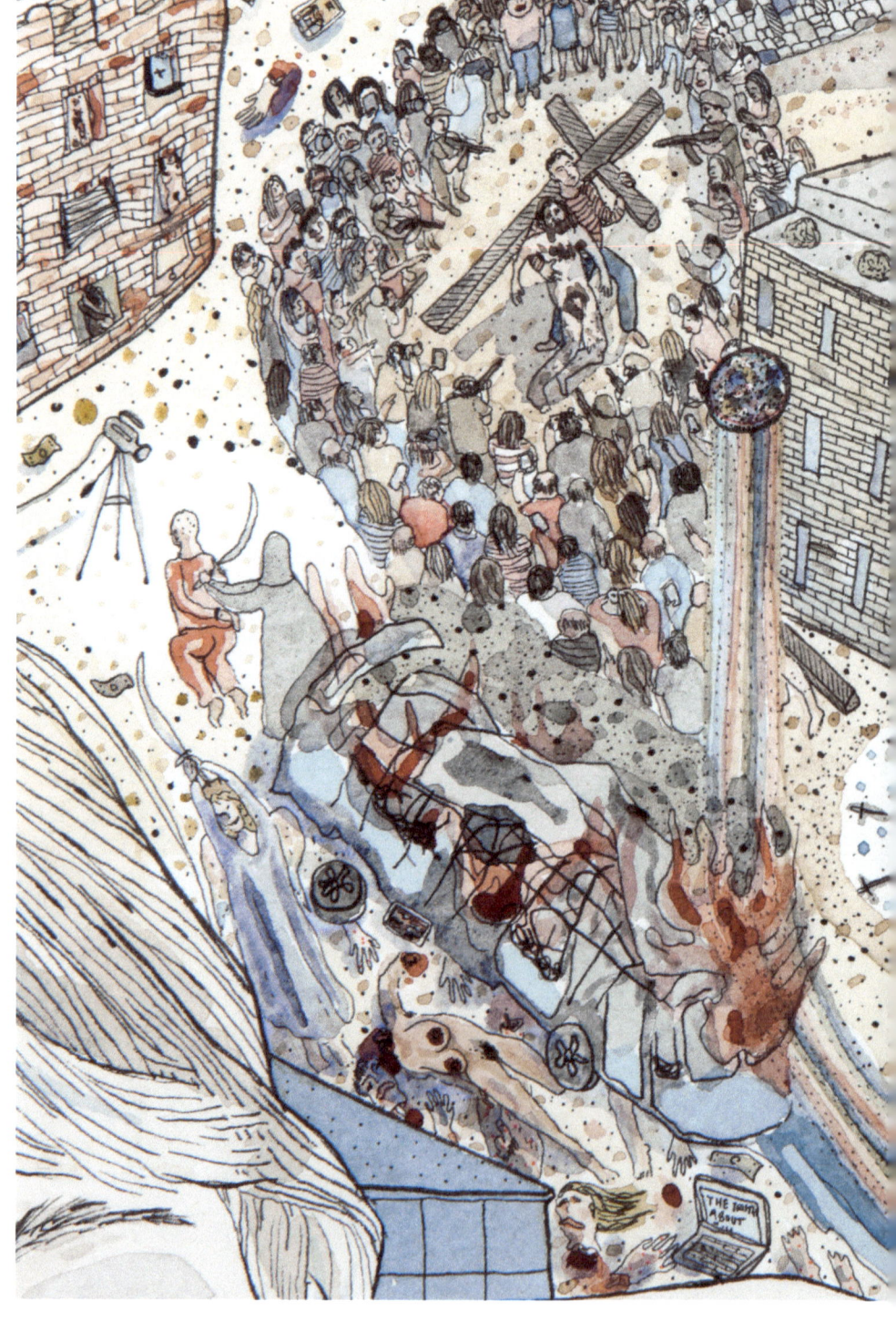

After this the Sanctum Sanctorum opened to my view and there stood the tabernacle witness to God's presence as the seven angels seven plagues holding emerged from within the temple clothed in purest linen glistening cinches of gold girding their chests and when one of the four living creatures handed the seven angels seven golden vials filled with the last wrath of YHWH the temple filled with the smoke of the glory and power of God none allowed to enter until the seven angels' seven plagues come to an end.

I heard a voice speak from within the temple saying to the seven angels, "Go! Pour out upon the Earth the seven vials filled with the wrath of God." So the first departed and poured his vial on the Earth. Grievous canker sores broke out on all who had the mark of the Son of Perdition and all who worshipped his image. The second poured his vial into the sea and it became as a dead man's blood, so that every soul died that dwelt upon the sea. The third angel poured his vial into the rivers and the springs and they too turned to blood.

Then I heard the angel of the waters say

> O Heilige, you are just in these your judgments,
>
> > you who were and truly are,
>
> for they spilled the blood of saints and prophets
>
> > and you gave them blood to drink, their just deserts.

Then too I heard the altar say

> Yea, Domine Deus Omnipotens,
>
> > just and righteous are all your judgments!

Then!

The fourth angel poured his vial over the sun and the sun scorched people with fire—but though blistered by the heat they cursed God's name for his power to plague them, turning not from their ways, not giving him glory. And so the fifth angel poured his vial right onto the throne of the beast plunging his kingdom to pitch darkness people gnawing their tongues in distress. Yet they swore at God in Heaven for their suffering and sores, still turning not from their ways. The sixth angel drained his vial upon the great River Euphrates, its waters drying up to make a pathway for the kings of the East. And I saw slytherin from the mouths of the serpent and the beast and the false prophet three spirits frog-green and foul—these are the spirits of sign-working demons spreading throughout the whole world gathering the kings of the Earth together for war in that great and terrible day of El Shaddai. Yet he says, "Behold, I come as a thief in the night. Blessed is she who keeps watch, who holds fast her garments lest she be found walking naked and they see her shame." And so they gathered themselves together near the place called in Hebrew Armageddon—which in English means Mount Megiddo.

Finally the seventh angel poured out his vial, this one into the air, and a voice boomed out from the temple and out from the throne declaring, "It is done!" And together there came lightning bolts voices thunder and a quaking tremulous roar such as never was no not from the ancient time man first walked upon the Earth now splitting in three the great city cratering the cities of the nations. For Babylon the Great has come up for remembrance before God, her time come to drink from the cup of wrath, the Tyrian-dark wine of his anger. All the islands fled; no mountain remained. Hailstones like crags fell grievous from the sky and the people cursed God for the harsh hailstone blows.

Now one of the seven angels having the seven flasks approached and spoke to me saying, "Come here and I will show you the judgment passed on the great slut sitting upon many waters, in whose bed Earth's kings reveled, Earth's people drunk with the wine of her lust." Then he carried me in the Spirit to the wilderness, where I saw a woman seated on a crimson beast. The beast was covered with curses and it had seven heads and ten horns. The woman was clothed in purple and scarlet encrusted with gold and gems and pearls holding in her hand a chalice filled to the brim with abominations and the filth of her desires and on her head was this name writ: "Mysterium, Babylon the Great, Mother of Whores and All Earthly Abominations." And I beheld the woman drunk with the blood of the saints, the blood of those martyred for Jesus the Great, Mother of Whores and All Earthly Abominations." And I beheld the woman drunk with the blood of the saints, the blood of those martyred for Jesus.

But I was dumbstruck at the sight of her. Then the angel said to me, "Why do you marvel. Let me explain to you the secret of the woman and of the beast with seven heads and ten horns that bears her. The beast you saw was but is no more and yet will rise from deep Hell's hollow to be destroyed. And all who inhabit the Earth seeing him will stand in awe— all those whose names have not been written in the Book of Life, even from the foundation of the world—because he was but is not and yet will come. Let this wisdom sink into your mind: The seven heads are the seven hills on which the woman sits. And the hills are seven kings. Of these, five have fallen, one still lives, and one is yet to come—and when he comes he must remain for some little time. And the Antichrist who was and is no more even he himself is the eighth. He springs from the seven—but he goes to destruction. Then too the ten horns you saw are ten kings.

They have not yet come into their kingdoms but when they do they will reign as kings along with the beast for the space of one hour. They will be of one mind and one heart. They will give their power and authority to the beast and they will wage war against the Lamb. But the Lamb will crush them to pieces, for he is Lord of Lords and King of Kings and those with him are called and chosen and faithful."

Again he spoke to me saying, "The waters you saw, where the great whore sits, are peoples and kin and nations and tongues. And the beast as well as the ten horns you saw will loathe the whore and lay her waste, leaving her naked, devouring her flesh, burning her with fire. For it is God who put it in their hearts so to unite in purpose, handing their kingdoms over to the beast, that God's own purposes might be fulfilled. And the whore you saw is that great city, the one that holds sway over all the kings of the Earth."

After these things I saw another angel descending from Heaven overwhelming in power, the Earth itself resplendent with his glory. He proclaimed with a voice of matchless strength

> Babylon is fallen! Babilônia that mighty city fallen
>
> > now become a den of demons
>
> guardhouse of every foul spirit
>
> > nest of every unclean bird
>
> lair of every vile and hated beast—
>
> > for Babylon was an aurelian cup in the Lord's hand
>
> and the nations drank the raging wine of her adultery,
>
> > Earth's kings, her lovers, reveling with her,

Earth's merchants gorged with the fat of her wealth,

    auri sacra fames.

But another voice from Heaven said,

    Come out from her, my people,

        that you share not in her sins

    neither in the woes she must suffer,

        for her sins are piled up to Heaven

    and God now calls her to account for her injustice.

        Give back to her as she has given,

pay her double according to her works,

        fill double the cup she herself has filled.

As much as she gloried in her own delights,

        just so let her measure be of torment and sorrow.

Because she said in her heart, "I reign as queen, no widow am I,

    I know no grief,"

so shall her sorrows come in a moment, a day—

        death, grief, famine—

and she will be consumed with fire,

        for the Lord God judging her is mighty.

The kings of the Earth, they who shared the delights of her bed, now shall weep and beat their breasts seeing her aflame and shall mourn wailing standing far off in fear lest they share her torment saying

> Alas, Babel, Βαβυλών, mighty city and strong,
>
> laid low in but an hour!

So too shall Earth's merchants wail over her and grieve, for no longer will any buy their wares—cargoes of gold from Ophir, silver from Tarshish, gemstones and pearls, fine linen from Egypt, dyed robes silken and crimson, scented woods from the East, horns of ivory and ebony, choice vessels of scented wood, brass, iron, marble, cinnamon and spice, myrrh and frankincense, Helbon wine, olives from Qana, market wheat of Minnith and Pannag, the cattle on a thousand hills, sheep and horses, Persian chariots, slave girls—and the souls of men. The very fruits your heart craved are wrenched from you, your fashions and splendor, all gone, not a feather to be found. And the traders and dealers enriched with these goods keep themselves far apart from her now, trembling wailing weeping in terror of her woes with nothing more to say than

> ¡Ay, ay, great Babilonia,
>
> > dressed in fine satin and lace
>
> purple and crimson
>
> > encrusted with gold
>
> gemstones and pearls—
>
> > sic transit gloria mundi!

They that go down to the sea in ships, that do business in great waters, they too stood afar off and cried seeing the smoke as she burned saying, "What city was ever like this great city?" Then they cast up dust upon their heads, wallowing themselves in the ashes, deep grieving, mourning, sighing in lamentation

> Hélas, Hélas Babylone la grande,
>
>> prospering ship captains and crew,
>
> in one hour your wealth is come to naught.

But the angel said, "Rejoice ye, O Heaven and saints, apostles and prophets! For God has brought judgment upon her for your sakes." And another mighty messenger lifted a stone, as it were a millstone, saying as he cast it into the sea

> Thus with violent rush
>
>> is that great city Babylon
>
> cast down to rise no more.
>
>> Taken away are the voice of mirth
>
> and the voice of gladness,
>
>> the voice of the bridegroom
>
> and the voice of the bride,
>
>> the grinding of the millstones
>
> and the light of the candle:
>
>> the rest is silence.
>
> For your merchants were Earth's great ones,

yet by your sorcery all the nations were deceived.

And so in her was found the blood of prophets, holy ones

and all those slaughtered upon the Earth.

After this the music of Heaven assembled singing

HAL-LE-LU-JAH!

Salvation and glory and power be to our God.

True and just are his judgments,

for he judged the great harlot,

she who seduced the whole world with her wiles,

he avenged the blood of his servants

spilled by her hand.

And a second time they sang

— and her smoke rose up ages on endless ages.

Then the twenty-four elders and the four living creatures fell down and worshipped before God seated upon his throne saying, "Aamen! Allelujah!" And a voice came forth from the throne saying

> Lodate il nostro Dio,
>
>> voi tutti suoi servitori.
>
> voi che lo temete,
>
>> piccolo e grandi.

Then I heard in myriad throng a multitude sing with rolling thunder

> Hallelujah!
>
>> for the Lord God Omnipotent reigneth!
>
> Gocémonos y alegrémonos y démosle gloria

> porque son venidas le nozze dell'Agnello
>
> and his bride se ha aparejado,
>
> robed in radiant linen, fine and pure—
>
> car le fin lin, ce sont les oeuvres justes des saints.

The angel said to me, "Write! Blessed are those who are called to the Lamb's wedding banquet." And again he said to me, "These are God's true words." At that I fell at his feet to worship him. But he said to me, "Gott bewahre! For I am but one of your brothers. We are fellow servants sharing the same witness to Jesus, to whom all prophecy testifies through the Spirit. Therefore worship not me, but God alone."

Then!

I saw Heaven opened and beheld one faithful and true seated on a white horse judging justly battling in righteousness eyes flaming as it were with fire on his head crowns and crowns engraved with names but written on his brow a new name known to him and none other his garment dipped in blood his name is called Ὁ Λόγος τοῦ Θεοῦ the Host of Heaven following him on white horses armies draped in linen gleaming pure as from his mouth with curved and slashing blade he goes subduing the nations ruling them with iron scepter trampling down the grapes of wrath stored in the winepress of the fury of God Almighty and on his garment and thigh this name wri. "King of Kings and Lord of Lords"—and before my eyes I saw within the sun an angel standing summoning all winged creatures flying through Heaven's midst with loud voice crying "Venez, rassemblez-vous! Gather yourselves on every side to God's great sacrifice on the mountains of Israel to feast on the flesh of captains and kings men of power horses riders the flesh of men both free and slave great and small."

Then I beheld the Antichrist the kings of the Earth their legions gathered together to war against the one seated on the throne and against his armies. But the beast was taken and with him the false prophet, the one who worked wonders wielding the beast's powers, deceiving all those sealed with the mark of the beast, worshipping his image—these two were tossed alive into a fiery lake, burning with sulphur. The rest were slain by the thrusting blade of the one seated on the white horse—and the birds gorged themselves with their flesh.

Yet another angel I saw descending from Heaven holding in his hand the key to the Deep Abyss and a mighty chain. He grabbed hold of the dragon, Old Scratch, that snake Satani, bound him for a thousand years, cast him into the Bottomless Pit and sealed it with lock and key, barring him for a thousand years from deluding the nations, until the millennium be passed. But after that, he must be loosed for a short while.

Then I saw thrones and those seated upon them given authority to judge. I saw too the souls of all beheaded for their witness to Jeziš and for the word of God and the souls of all those who had not worshipped the beast or his image neither taken his seal upon their foreheads or their hands—these all rose from the dead to reign a thousand years with Messiah. But the rest of the dead did not live again until the millennium had passed. This is the first resurrection. Blessed and holy are those who have a share in the first resurrection—the second death has no power over them, but they shall be priests of God and his Anointed and reign a thousand years with him.

Yet when the thousand years are up the Wicked One will be freed from his prison and go out to deceive the nations in the four corners of the Earth, even Gog the prince of Magog, to gather them together to war their number as the sands of the sea coming like a storm cloud shadowing the land encircling the camp of the saints and the beloved city—

but fire streamed down on them from Heaven, consuming them utterly. And that Father of Lies, the Serpent of Old, he was cast into the lake of fire burning with sulphur there tormented with the Man of Sin and the false prophet day and night, evermore.

Then I saw a great white throne. Earth and Heaven fled from the presence of him that sat upon it—there was no place for them any longer. Then too I saw the dead, both great and small, standing before the throne. The books were opened, and another book, Bók Lífsins, and the dead were judged according to all that was written in the books, according to their deeds. The sea yielded up its dead and Death and Hell yielded up the dead in them. Each one was judged according to his deeds. Then Doom and Destruction themselves were cast into the flaming lake. This is the second death. But if anyone was not found written in the Book of Life he too was pitched into Gehenna's blaze, where maggots never die and sulphur burns forever, unconsumed.

I saw a new Heaven and new Earth—for the first Heaven and the first Earth had disappeared and the sea was no more. I saw New Jerusalem the holy city coming down out of Heaven, from God himself, prepared as a bride is adorned for her husband. I heard a voice in might from Heaven say, "Behold, God's tabernacle is with mankind and he shall abide in their midst and they will be his people and God himself will be with them. He will wipe away every tear from their eyes, he will swallow up death in victory, there will be no more pain or weeping or suffering—for the things that were no longer are."

He that sat upon the throne said, "Look! I have made everything new." And he said, "Write! For these words are faithful and true." Then he said to me, "It is done. Eu sou o Alfa e o Ômega, no início e no final. I will give to all who are thirsty freely to drink from the fountain of the Water of Life. Whoever overcomes will inherit all things: I will be his God and he will be my son. But the cowardly and faithless the hateful and murderers lechers sorcerers idolaters—and all who lie—these have their share in Gehenna's brimstone basin. This is the second death."

One of the seven angels who had one of the vials with one of the seven last plagues came and spoke to me saying, "Come up here! I will show you the Bride, the wife of the Lamb." He carried me on in the Spirit to a towering lofty peak and showed me the holy city, Jerusalén, coming down out of Heaven from God himself, having his splendor, her radiance like that of crystalline jasper her roof in grandeur soaring. There were twelve gates to the city with twelve angels watching and upon the gates the names graven were the twelve tribes of Israel—three gates in the East three gates in the North three gates in the South three gates in the West. And in the wall of the city twelve foundation stones were laid and upon them were etched the names of the Lamb's twelve apostles.

The angel who spoke to me held a golden measuring rod to measure the city and her gates and her wall. The city lay foursquare, length and width the same. He measured the city with the rod—fifteen hundred miles per side—length and breadth and height all equal. He measured the depth of the wall as well, 144 cubits in a man's terms (also that of the angel), some 200 feet. The wall seemed built of green jasper, the city itself pellucid gold, transparent, pure, the foundation stones adorned with jewels—the first jasper, the second sapphire, the third chalcedony, the fourth emerald, the fifth sardonyx, the sixth carnelian, the seventh tourmaline, the eighth beryl, the ninth topaz, the tenth green agate, the eleventh jacinth, the twelfth amethyst—and the twelve gates twelve pearls each fashioned from a single pearl opening to golden streets pure like glass.

But I saw no temple in the city, for the Lord God, Ὁ Παντοκράτωρ, he is its temple, he and the Lamb. Neither was there sun nor moon in its vaulted sky, for the city is lit by God's lambent glory, the Lamb its ever-

lasting radiance. The nations come to its brightness, bringing the wealth of the seas. The city's gates are not shut by day and there is no night. Within it lie all nations' praise and honor. Nothing unclean or detestable shall be found in it neither any lie, and those alone may enter whose names are written in the Lamb's Book of Life.

Then he showed me a river of living water lucent as polished glass flowing from the throne of God and the Lamb. In the midst of the city's street and on both sides of the river stood the Tree of Life. It bore twelve kinds of fruit, yielding its fruits every month. And the leaves of the tree were for healing of the nations. There will be nothing cursed in the city, for in it is the throne of God and the Lamb and there will his people serve him. They will see his face. His name will be on their foreheads. Night shall be no more neither shall they need any lamp nor the light of the sun–for the Lord God himself shines upon them. And they shall reign forever and ever, ages without end.

He said to me, "These words are faithful and true: The Lord God sent his messenger, imbued with the spirits of the prophets, to reveal to his servants the things that soon must be."

"Behold, I am coming quickly. Blessed is she who guards the words of the prophecy of this book."

It was I John who heard and saw these things. And when I had seen and heard I fell down to worship at the feet of the angel who showed me all this. But he said to me, "God forbid! I am just one of your brothers, a fellow servant with you and the prophets and all those who keep safe the words of this book. Therefore worship God alone." Then he said, "Seal not the prophetic words of this book–for the moment is upon us. Let him who does wrong yet do wrong; let him who is foul yet be foul; but let him who is just yet do what is right; and let him who is holy yet be holy."

"Behold, I am coming quickly and I have everyone's pay, to give to each according to his deeds. Ik ben alfa en omega, het begin en het einde, de eerste en de laatste. Blessed are those whose long robes have been cleansed, so shall they eat of the Tree of Life and enter the holy city. Outside are the treyf—sorcerers libertines assassins idolaters—and all those who love to tell lies. I Jesús have sent my messenger to testify these things to you for the sake of the churches. Io sono la radice e il ramo di David, inizio splendente dell'alba."

The Spirit and the Bride say "Come" and let all who hear say "Come" and let all who are thirsty come to the river and all who desire drink freely the Water of Life.

I charge you now, you who hear the words of the prophecy of this book: If anyone adds to these words God will heap on him the plagues here written and if anyone takes away from the words written in the book of this prophecy God will take away his share of the Tree of Life, out from the holy city. The one who bears witness to these things says, "Truly I come quickly."

Michael Straus was born and raised in New Jersey and, after a number of years practicing law in New York, undertook graduate studies in classical languages there and in England. He currently lives in Alabama where he is intermittently engaged in translations from Greek, such as this volume, as well as Spanish, including previously untranslated poems of Pablo Neruda. Apart from those activities, he is actively involved in the work of various museums and artist foundations.

Jennifer May Reiland was born in Texas and raised in the shadow of the End Times. She studied art at Cooper Union and lives and works in New York City. She has been awarded residencies at the Sharpe-Walentas Studio Program; the Fondation des Etats-Unis as a Hale Woolley Scholar; and the Drawing Center's Open Sessions program. She has yet to escape the threat of the End Times.

www.ingramcontent.com/pod-product-compliance
Lightning Source LLC
Chambersburg PA
CBHW042234090526
44588CB00005B/74